DISPATCHES FROM

THE
SWINGING DOOR
SALOON

**Poems from my 10-year bender
inside heaven's dive bar**

RANDALL MCNAIR

B S
Bits of Steak Press
Alameda, CA

Previous publication information about some of the poems contained within this work can be found on page V.

ISBN paperback: 978-1-7351080-0-1
ISBN ebook: 978-1-7351080-1-8

Printed in the United States of America

Cover design by Graye Smith
Edited by Caesar Kent
Interior typesetting by Vanessa Mendozzi

Publisher's Cataloging-In-Publication Data
(Prepared by The Donohue Group, Inc.)

Names: McNair, Randall, author.
Title: Dispatches from the Swinging Door Saloon : poems from my 10-year bender inside heaven's dive bar / Randall McNair.
Description: Alameda, CA : Bits of Steak Press, [2020]
Identifiers: ISBN 9781735108001 (paperback) | ISBN 9781735108025 (hardcover) | ISBN 9781735108018 (ebook)
Subjects: LCSH: Life--Poetry. | Death--Poetry. | American poetry. | LCGFT: Humorous poetry. | Poetry.
Classification: LCC PS3613.C58574 D57 2020 (print) | LCC PS3613.C58574 (ebook) | DDC 811/.6--dc23

This book is dedicated to my beautiful wife Lisa, whose endurance during this 10-year bender is the stuff of legend. Thank you, my blobbed for sticking around and encouraging me to write. It was you who told me about my first poetry workshop down in Key West with Sharon Olds back in 2002. And it was you who told me about my most recent workshop with Billy Collins in Southampton, NY, in 2019.

Additionally, I would like to acknowledge and thank the aforementioned poets, Sharon Olds and Billy Collins, for their support of my writing. Their keen eye for detail and tremendous wit have helped me hone my craft and tidy the poems in this book.

Finally, here's a tilt of the mug to Charles Bukowski whose countless books of poetry kept me company on many a barstool during this decade-long bender.

Cheers to the lot o' ye!

ACKNOWLEDGMENTS

Grateful acknowledgment is made to the editors of the following periodicals, where these poems first appeared, some in slightly different versions:

Blood & Bourbon #6: "Dispatches from the Swinging Door Saloon," "Baffling St. Peter I Make it Into Heaven," and "Feeling a bit Uncomfortable"

Rip Rap, Spring 2002: "Writer Passes"

I would also like to acknowledge the following sponsors of my Kickstarter campaign, without whom this book would still be stuck in a drawer or tucked in the margins of a book somewhere.

WATERFORD DECANTED MIDLETON VERY RARE
SILENT DISTILLERY LEVEL SPONSORS ($500+)

The Baumer Family, Dr. Patrick McNair & my brothers, Thomas McNair, Ronald McNair, & Scott McNair.

TEQUILA GOLD LEVEL SPONSORS ($250-$500)

Mike Lockwood, Rick Quast, Michael "Mick" Jerding,
Maureen "Mojo" O'Flaherty, and my parents, Dick &
Marge McNair

Thank you, one and all, for your extraordinary generosity
here in the middle of a global pandemic!

Contents

On Musing

On Loving

On Living

On Dying

DISPATCHES FROM

THE
SWINGING DOOR
SALOON

Looking into the mirror

of what once was

all one can do

is reflect.

On Working

My $50/Yr. Job

I am working
a $50/yr. job.

It is called poetry.

It makes for
tough living.

But then,
when was living
ever easy?

THE BANKER

It's hard to find the will
to shave. Brushing my teeth
is a pointless chore. I shower,
but even that seems like folly.

I do not work in the fields
or in the coal mines
or deep in the sewers.
I work in an air-conditioned
cube at the bank.

I do not sweat or gather grime
as I sit here, cleanly,
making money move
this way or that,
my jaw moving
up and down and side to side,
my eyes cloudy and blank.

I am a banker.

It's hard to find the will
for many, many things.

IT'S THE FIRE'S FAULT

The hills above Irvine are on fire,
over 3,500 acres plowed by flame.
There is ash falling but
no sign of the birds, no blue
to the sky. You can't fight
these things. Best to give in,
cut out of the office early,
have a beer or two or twelve
at the Swinging Door Saloon,
tell your manager
when you show up late
for the meeting tomorrow
that it's the fire's fault,
and maybe he should have
pushed the deadline back until
the sparrows have resumed their singing
and the pall is erased from the sky.

THE MAD SCIENTIST

Drunk on wine,
your old man misses Kennedy's space speech
there at Rice University.

You can't blame him though.

Old Man's been waiting for so long,
even the most vigilant would have given up.
So, as he lies on the powder blue sofa
slowly angering at your dog's easy life,
Kennedy delivers the goods
to a moderate crowd of Texans,
LBJ in the audience smirking,
as if aware of things to come.

Old Man, wake up, you want to say,
but you also want to let the bugger
lie there, sleep it off,
wake up at noon the next day
and see it in print,
his idea made word
fresh off the President's lips.

Yes, let him wake up slow and queasy,
gagging at his toothbrush
as his transistor radio

says something about the moon.

Let him drop his guts in the hallway
as he rushes to the kitchen for the paper
and, as he grabs it out of your hands,
knocking over your bowl of cereal,
look up at him and remember that face,
glorious and smiling,
crazed as the day you were born.

A Quick Story About the Strangest Politician I Ever Met

He changed his name from
Jackson P. Falldrecker to Bart Linklater
hoping to connect with the older crowd.

He was thirty-seven with silver hair
and an artificial hip. He wore plaid
trousers, white leather shoes,
and fat ties made of orange polyester
over blue and red checkered shirts.

It was his midlife and golden years
all at once. He cashed in his retirement
and ordered a 70-year-old virgin
from Romania to keep him company.
They moved to Florida
to a sleepy senior community
near Osceola.

Nadia, his bride, got a pair
of 38 double D's and a face lift
and helped Bart campaign
for president of the Fading Willows
Homeowners Association.

They made buttons and bumper stickers,

threw parties by the pool at 1pm,
sponsored bus rides to Sizzler
and field trips to the post office.

Bart won by a landslide,
got his face in the papers
and a key to the city. Then,
on the day of his installation,
he choked on an olive and died.

MUSIC MAKER

I fancy myself to be the piano player
in a 19th century saloon in some dusty,
old farming town—Albuquerque
let's say, or Tustin, California.
And, as I sit there getting drunk on
whiskey and beer, straw hat cocked
atop my head, little black garter
wrapped around the left bicep
of my red-and-white-striped,
long-sleeved shirt, the spittoon
at my feet slowly filling, my hands
diligently going about their work
of making music fill the room with life,
some joker in his man-blouse walks up
to the juke and plays Lady Gaga,
cutting me out of that scene
and pasting me back into this one,
where I sit beneath my baseball cap
getting drunk on whiskey and beer,
staring at the little black garter
around the bargirl's leg as I spit spent
sunflower shells into my Carl's Jr. cup,
my hands diligently going about
their work of making music fill
the pages of my notebook with life.

THE BURNOUT

I was at the game.
It was a 12:35pm start.
It is now 12:35am and
I am hammered.

I had cut out
of the office early,
my phone ringing,
a client waiting in the lobby.

It's April, baby, and I had tickets
to the game.

Fuck work, anyway.
Fuck it in April, May, June
and July. Fuck it big time in August
and September. Don't even think about work
in October, as the leaves begin to fall
nor in November and December—
a time for feasting with family.

January is too cold for work.
February too rainy.
Fuck work in January and February.
This leaves March.
Only in March should one work,

though never on St. Patrick's Day
nor for two weeks before or after.

BRUNIE BLOWSME

The porn star named himself
Rod Givermore
on account of him thinking
it was both clever and true.

And his coworkers
are all 9's and 10's
so I tell my boss I am quitting
and I ride down into the valley
on a smoking, 17-year-old
brunette named Patty Pinay
and announce my new name—
Brunie Blowsme.

If not for the blistering,
the itching,
and the federal warrant
for my arrest,
I could very well be
the next big thing.

AT WORK IN THE BANK

Do I look as miserable
as I feel, sitting here in this
high-backed, leather chair?

Here, where Hope's head was cleaved
open just yesterday, after a short
lunch meeting at my desk?

Curious,
I steal a peek
in the mirror.

No.
The answer is
no.

My eyes are not bleeding
and there is no hatchet
wedged into my forehead.

On Writing

Monkey See

Monkey C,
Baboon A.
Baboon studied harder.

A Quick Note About Hope

I don't write with hope.
I do it with pen and paper
and a tired, open mind.
People suggest adding some hope to my poems
so the reader can leave with something.
I say let the reader leave
empty handed—
it's the only way I can be sure
I've conveyed myself truthfully.

And Here I Thought I Had

You never write love poems.
It's always beer and bargirls
and the breaking of bones.

You know, you could throw in
a sonnet once in a while, or a haiku
about the deep pools of my eyes.

I wait for that, but nothing.
Just endless musings about
your dead relatives,

frigid beer in frosty mugs,
the Swinging Door Saloon,
bar fights, Bukowski, brunettes.

Love poems. You really should write
some goddam love poems!

JOHNNY MCMURPHY

I am a salesman and my tired eyes
and weak wisp of hair say more than
my condensed sales pitch ever will.

I'm broke. Depressed.
Haven't been to the Door in 37 days
and my poetry sucks.

Also, I have gout.

So, to bring the élan back I take to writing fantasies
on old cocktail napkins found tucked into my pockets,
and in the margins of my beer-stained books.

Today, I am Johnny McMurphy,
a wealthy Irish whiskey tycoon,
with an abnormally large cock (for an Irishman),
and I am sitting by the fire in the first of the more
than eighteen pubs I bought upon coming to America.
My Filipina wife is knitting me a beer cozy back home,
while drunk blonde girls from Simi Valley
poke each other in the eyes with acrylic nails
for the right to blow me. The steak I am eating
is imported from the beef country of Japan
and my Bentley, which caught fire twelve weeks ago
due to my crack problem, is now out of the shop.

Furthermore, Santa Claus has me on his Nice List,
the angels have whispered into the Pope's ear
and he has created a holy day in my honor,
and my dead kin are dancing on the bar
as if nothing ever happened.

God only knows what tomorrow will bring.

WRITER'S BLOCK

I sit in my study
taking stock—
the books,
the gathering of dust,
the slant of bookshelf,
the jigger of whiskey
beneath the brass lamp.

It all fits; even I fit,
and this computer,
and the ballads playing overhead
by Springsteen and Bad Company
and the Young Dubliners.

Everything is as it should be.

But the computer screen is blank,
and my mind,
and all across the room
there is no hope,
no gleaming white saint
sitting in a chair
nodding his affirmation.

There is just a room
full of dusty books I did not write,

a bookshelf that will need repair,
and a jigger of whiskey which,
like the others before it,
promises nothing.

LA-Z-POEMS

Not every poem comes
bounding out, a first grader
at the recess bell.
Some prefer to mold themselves
into the soft, suede recliner,
remote wedged into one palm,
a beer warming in the other.
If they move at all, it's for
the short trip to the fridge—
that sandwich parts factory
and keeper of the ales.

On rare occasions, a lone poem
will drag himself upstairs,
dropping crumbs and spilling beer.

He'll take one look at me
behind my computer and frown,
like a child grounded
in the middle of baseball season.

He'll plop down in the beanbag
at the foot of my desk,
eating his meal off his lap,
pouting but present.

We'll sit there together for hours
struggling for words,
a couple of sullen teens,
poem and poet alike
hunched and moping.

On Punctuation

Forget the comma,
that little busybody.
I propose a toast to
the unfettered line
gleeful and whistling
as it speeds along in its roadster
flicking cigarette ash out the window
blowing red lights
sending semicolons
and asterisks
scrambling for cover
as the forgotten comma,
stiff-lipped and proper,
directs traffic in
the intersection,
its whistle blaring,
its little white gloves
ordering everything
to a halt,
everything but the rogue line
which speeds
headlong into
the night
its long hair
blowing in the wind
its yee-haws and hell-yeahs

echoing down alleyways
and into young ladies' ears
as they dance in their kitchens
alone
drinking wine from the bottle
their parentheses
jiggling in their blouses
their imaginations carrying them away
to bedrooms full of exclamation points
far away from this nagging fear
about missed periods
and that lazy brotherhood
of potbellied question marks
known as their husbands.

ALMOST, BUT NOT QUITE

The problem with perfection is that
it's almost harder to deconstruct
or learn from than failure.

Take one of Billy Collins's poems for example,
the jersey of its page cleanly pressed, unstained
by mustard, or cheese, or buttered popcorn,
each stanza beautifully seated in the bleachers,
the little cap of its title worn squarely atop its head,
its team of metaphors All Star caliber,
each line a frozen rope over third base,
each word choice a grand slam
crushed over the center field wall.

What can one say but *Wow!*
or *Holy shit, did you see that?!*

Compare that with my own work,
a veritable encyclopedia
of what-not-to-do-when-writing-poetry,
my stanzas ugly and teetering (drunks at 2am),
my metaphors a mixed bag
of potpourri and mulch, my lines more like
skid marks on the inside of your underwear,
my word choices hanging like limp dicks
in a porn flick. My work is so chock full

of lessons it is almost inspiring.
Almost, but not quite—
like a drunk's chances in life,
like a limp-dicked pornstar's prospects of getting paid,
like a textbook written in rhyme,
or a book of poetry dotted with asterisks
and filled with footnotes pointing
the reader to supporting documentation,
like this poem's hopes of making it
into print and finding its way
into an anthology of the world's best poetry—
almost, but not quite.

Dispatches From the Swinging Door Saloon

Today at 12pm sharp, the boy will arrive
on his imaginary horse, jumping down
from the stirrups with a jingling of spurs
and a flapping of chaps.

He'll remove his hat, wipe the sweat off
his brow with the sleeve of his long, brown,
leather coat, grab the satchel from around
the horse's neck and head inside the dark bar.

I sit in the corner finishing one last poem—this one
about a pantry full of glowing thoughts, which I store
there in glass jars that fill the shelves like a hundred
little candles burning in the alcove of an old church.

He'll tip his hat to the pretty bargirl
and mosey on over to the empty stool beside me,
where a freshly poured beer and a shot
of whiskey sit waiting atop the bar for his arrival.

He'll hit the shooter first,
then the beer (as he always does), and then
he'll gather up my cocktail napkins
and shovel them into his bag.

He'll flip a silver dollar to the bargirl,

pat me on the back and,
grabbing his bag off the bar,
he'll head back into the daylight.

Once outside, he'll mount his horse
and gallop away, beginning his 2,000-mile
journey to St. Joseph, Missouri, with a firing
of his pistol and a hearty "He-YAW!"

He will then commence a series of 10-mile sprints,
stopping at each interval just long enough to
switch horses, sip some water from his canteen,
and then continue on his way.

At nightfall, he'll make camp and, though he swore
an oath, he'll pull a bottle of Oklahoma moonshine
from the other side of his satchel and take a few hits,
before settling in to read my stuff beside the fire.

In a couple weeks, he will be 18
and the Express won't need him
anymore, so he focuses on one of my
coming of age tales—

the one about a young Pony Express rider who left
Tustin, California, one Tuesday in the dead
of summer, arriving two weeks later
in St. Joseph, Missouri, a fully-grown man.

ON DRINKING

It is Beautiful

I view the world
through
beer-filled glasses
and it is
beautiful!

MY 30 OUNCE WORLD

Thick glass, frosty dew dripping
along the outside,
a little frozen beer pond on top
where tiny Filipinas
skate around in white boots
and bikinis.

And below the ice,
a flyspeck apartment
where two microscopic beer people
make love to Van Morrison's
"Into the Mystic,"
whispering promises they won't keep.

And below them, a crowded discotheque
with minuscule bubble people
in their tightest silks
bouncing up and down,
their little groins gyrating to
the latest Jennifer Lopez song.

I watch the entire society there
in my beer, then swallow everyone
in one giant tilt of the mug.
I stare at the emptiness for a moment
then ask the guy next to me,

Fuck, buddy, did you see that?!

A Poem Ending in Cliche

The man at the Mission
showed me a poem they found
written on a cocktail napkin and
crumpled in the pocket of my slacks:

Christ, how I long for a midday drink—
to leave work early on a Wednesday
and hit a dark bar with
more women than men on the stools.
I want to spill Powers
down the end of my chin
and wipe it with the sleeve of my suit.
I want to drink my way to charming,
then to sexy, then to obnoxious
and foul, and I want to get
kicked out alone and take a header
into my colleague's Mercedes and
watch his wife shrink in fear.
I want to wake up bleeding in the dirt
beneath some roses
in an upscale neighborhood, my tie
stained and chunky with puke.
I want to wake up jobless
homeless
and alone.

Upon feeding and praying over me
the Reverend put his arm around me
and walked me outside. He gave
me a Bible and some advice:

Son, he said, *it is right to
bring your petitions to the Lord—
but I implore you,
be careful what you wish for.*

PRIORITIES

Last month,
I spent more on whiskey and beer
at the Swinging Door Saloon
than I did getting my ear looked at
by the ENT specialist.
And, Lord knows,
I got more enjoyment from the liquor
than any doctor visit ever,
although I do wish my ear wasn't still
so fucked up.

Today,
I should get this cavity filled.
That would feel nice.
No more metallic ache
fouling up my meals.
But that $120
is the equivalent of 20 tall beers
at the Door.

Needless to say, I choose those.

I know, you're right.
I could have just ten tall ones
and start a savings account for the tooth,
but I am 42 years old

and I am broke—savings accounts
do not last long around me.
I would probably end up with 15 beers
and 8 hamburgers
and the tooth still would not be fixed.

I am a smart man.
I will let the tooth
decay into a powdery nub,
allowing the bacteria to add to
my beer buzz. That will be
the equivalent of 25.5 beers,
a far better use of funds
given my current circumstances.

And please, don't bother
lecturing me on my priorities.
I couldn't hear you
if I wanted to,
and I don't.

WET DOG

The AA meeting lets out early
and the non-drunk
former drunks
file down the steps
discussing the god force
and redemption.

I try to avoid them.

They are swell people,
don't get me wrong.
But sometimes a wet dog
just wants to be a wet dog,
without being reminded
that he is a wet dog.

WHAT'S A FELLA GOTTA DO?

Getting a beer in this place
is like having
your gums probed
by a drunk dentist
with fat, filthy fingers!
I yell to anyone.

Johnny, and Big Dave, and 240
and Sean O' stare at me like
I just stuck a hand up their mom's skirt,
and 240 speaks up
on behalf of the group,
Huh? What the fuck? he says.

So, I apologize—
for the yelling, but not for the sentiment—
and I push my way to the front of the bar
bumping shoulders and nudging elbows.
And all the metrosexuals in their
low-cut jeans, and flowery man-blouses,
and rooster-dos, and little patches
of chin-hair are dropping their daiquiris
and wine coolers all over the place,
throwing angry glares at me
while back at our table my pals
are finishing their whiskey

and planning their escape.

But it's too late—
a fist comes flying over
the top of everything
connecting squarely with the back of my head
and I turn and knuckle the first asshole
I see, and it's game on!
And my buddies and I are in it shoulder
to shoulder, and glass is breaking, and bones,
and suddenly I am at the bottom of a pile
and there, next to my cheek, is a full,
ice-cold bottle of beer and, reaching out,
I think *Goddamn, it's about time!*

UNFORCED, UNPROVOKED AND UNBELIEVABLE

The lights
keep flashing and the wheels
keep turning and I
keep getting drunk and the social workers
keep chipping away and the wife
keeps challenging me and the cat
keeps killing and my conscience
keeps pacing its dark motel room
and the beautiful women,
brown skin, black hair,
bodies—they
keep showing up for work.

So it is in my world,
all this wild, sloppy living,
unforced, unprovoked
and unbelievable.

HILLARY! HILLARY! COME MEET MY FRIENDS!

It's 5:30pm and the beer camp
has just ended. Hillary is here.
Time for me to go.
I don't have much in life
but I have this dark bar
and a quiet stool in the corner
(or I did have that, before Hillary).
And I'll be damned
if I am going to sit here
with my whiskey shooter and beer
getting squeezed on both sides
while Hillary and her friends
sticky up the joint with their spilled drinks
and sappy shouting.

A man is well served to know his limits
and Hillary is mine.

MISUNDERSTANDING

Put out the light, she says
as she climbs into bed.
So I take the lamp out
into the yard
and plug it in beneath the begonias.
Beautiful! I think,
as my wife calls her parents
to see if it would be alright
to bring the kid and stay awhile and I,
grinning in the garden at midnight,
crack open a beer and wait.

What to Look for While Drinking with Me

Elves, halitosis, shivers, brunettes,
   your hands, your car keys, your wallet,
breasts, people without eyes,
         ears or necks. You should look
   out for my dead relatives,
haberdashers, whores (look hard
   for whores, they love being
         discovered). Look out for anthrax,
baby teeth, turtles, flying monkeys,
   witches, drug pushers, orange eaters,
         cripples, talking tigers,
the dentist. If you see him,
tell him you're doing fine
         and you've been meaning to call.
You can look for an answer,
   but don't expect to find it.
         You have a better chance
of finding college students who
want to fuck.
   Look for them, by the way,
that's good stuff. Look for potato sacks,
apple crates, disco balls,
         pumas, coffee grinds,
bloody knuckles. Look for whatever
   you like. Just please do not come
looking for me. I am passed out beneath

the tournefortia

alone,

and I kind of like it this way.

Swinging Door Saloon, Wednesday 2pm

You and I, we're in the same boat,
he says to his buddy.
His buddy is 26
with a smoking-hot, 24-year-old girlfriend.
Yeah, I'm 64 and my wife is 50.
She idolizes me
and disrespects me all at once.
He kills his shot
and takes a deep tug of his beer.
So, anyway, she has this way
of looking at me
that makes me uncomfortable,
like I am losing my balance or something.
What the fuck, he says,
I'm out there every day
looking for work!
It's not like I'm sitting on my ass all day
doing nothing, you know?
He orders two more for his buddy and him.
So the bitch just smiles an' says,
"I know, Honey." in her broken English,
"I know, you're the best."
The shots come; they devour the shots.
Then he continues, *So I tell her,*
"Look, you stupid immigrant,
I had money. I spent so much

47

on attorney's fees
and your fucking green card,
there's just nothing left."
He orders two more.
His buddy's cellphone rings.

His buddy holds up his finger
and answers
before standing and exiting the bar.

Finally, some peace
and goddam quiet.

A Vow

The flying monkeys have
shat upon my book
and the Chiquita Banana girl
is dancing atop the bar,
chucking fruit at me and singing,
I'm Chiquita Banana and I'm here to say,
is this really any way to spend your day?
So I quit drinking
for 5 minutes and 34 seconds
as I head to the pisser,
and as I cross the parking lot
for the outhouse, from nowhere
the Partridge Family and
the Brady Bunch
come barreling down on me,
their buses pulsing with disco lights
and naked go-go dancers,
and just as I begin to run
screaming like a scared goat
they sound their horns
and flash their grins
and vanish into thin air.

Sweating and a bit shaken
I move on, have my piss,
shake, put it away, exit,

look both ways,
cross the parking lot
back to the dive bar, elucidated,
knowing now that even
5 minutes and 34 seconds
of non-drinking
can create hallucinations
and irrational behavior
and I vow to be more
vigilant
from here on out.

I Apologize

The hummingbird
fluttering into my
peripheral vision
was really just
a napkin caught
in the roses,
which reminds me
of the haiku I once wrote:

> *The raisin I watched*
> *tumble into my oatmeal*
> *was really a fly.*

Also, I am very drunk
and I apologize
for wasting your time
with these pointless musings.

HANGOVER HAIKU

To the King, the Queen,
to the executioner:
PLEASE, OFF WITH MY/

HEAD!

ON MUSING

At Last! Here is the Answer to Life's Eternal Question.

D. All of the above

CHARM

You don't put Charm in your lunchbox
and take him with you to work.
This is frivolous and wasteful of his time
and he will not stand for it.
But, if you are lucky, when you need him,
he will hail a taxi
and race across town to your flat,
Italian bread in one hand
a bottle of Chianti in the other.
And just as you find yourself
at a loss for words
he will drop the food on the table
and leap into your mouth
and, while your date is looking to leave,
Charm will begin dancing on your tongue
and your date will notice
and find him cute
and she will make herself comfortable
and remove her heels
and she will ask to sit in the beanbag
and do you have any Lionel Richie
and what a beautiful painting,
wherever did you find it?

And Charm, seeing the fruits of his labor
will float a story about

a golden retriever you saved
from the pound
an hour before he was to be put down,
and the date with one foot out the door
is now the date with naked ankles
dangling from your beanbag,
wine spilling from her glass,
mischief in her eyes
and, if you're not mistaken,
a hint of wetness on her panties
which, by the good grace of Charm,
are beginning to show beneath her skirt.

A MAN'S TIME

A man's time is a man's time.
Respect it. Do not coach him
on its use. Do not wallpaper
your yellow wallpaper over it.

Do not cover it with rugs
or splash it with holy water.
Do not chuck darts at it
or throw beer in its face.

Do not cook it meatloaf
and lima beans in an attempt
to win it over.
It is his time.

Let him burn it
at the stake
or stick it
with pins.

Let him watch it
drift away in a dingy
as he lies drunk
on the beach.

It is not your place to speak

to a man's time any more than it is
your place to mount a man's horse
and disappear into the desert.

A man's time is a man's time.
Accept it for what it is.
If you do, he may just
adorn it in gold and give it to you.

ABSORBING THE LOCAL CULTURE

She suggested we try
to absorb the local culture
so I cut a long slit across my belly
and began shoving in small children
and ancient vases
and assorted old ladies
and their various tea parties
and their flowery, porcelain teacups,
and I would wait until
the stomach acid had cleared room,
and I would add local sports teams
and clergymen
and tuba players,
and I put the mayor in there
and absorbed him down
to his last $300 shoe,
and I absorbed that too,
and then my girl said something rude
so I shoved her in there
with an angry manhandling,
and now I am very knowledgeable
about the ways of this place,
even as my loneliness swells
and my stomach grows awfully upset.

THE FALLDRECKERS

I have created a family name—Falldrecker.
Google it and you will find nothing.
So, I whip out a quick genealogy
with drunk uncles found dead in the snow
and handsome aunts who proved crucial
to women's suffrage,
and the whole story is quite compelling.

But FamilyTree.com comes calling
and says it's all a fraud
and they begin removing Falldreckers
one by one, starting at the top
with Phineas C., the first known Falldrecker—
born in Berlin in the mid 1800s
to unknown parents and rumored
to be descended from Charlemagne himself.
Then down to his son,
Jackson P., born in 1899 in a small village
on the outskirts of Munich
on a cold December day.
And soon they have erased the whole lot—
Jackson the 2nd, son of Jackson P.,
a man with a ferocious temper and severe
drinking problem, and Charles his 3rd born,
who, like his father was a mean drunk,
taking a barmaid by the hips one evening,

placing inside her a little girl, Gertrude.
Then they remove Gertrude
and before you know it,
the poor Falldrecker clan dies off again,
returning to the lips of a lone German
on the outskirts of Munich who says,
while gutting a fish in the local market,
THIS is what we do to Falldreckers!

FEELING A BIT UNCOMFORTABLE

They invited me onto their boat
so they could throw me off it.
That's okay, they always
kept the hull full of beer
and I do know how to swim.
But as I looked around
I noticed rope and an extra anchor.
There was a shark stunner
and harpoon, though I could
certainly understand those.
But there was a hacksaw too,
and books on disposing of bodies
and a large tub of hydrochloric acid
and a clipboard with my name
on it, and little pictures of me
with a thick red line through
the middle, and the devil was there
handing out $100 bills and
the saints I pray to were
taking the money and my dear,
sweet, dead grandmother
was sitting on the bow giving
me the finger and suddenly
I began to feel a bit uncomfortable
even though I knew how to swim
and was on a boat with a hull full of beer.

On Loving

The Saddest, Quickest Phone Call I Ever Received

I just called to say I love you
and don't come home.

20TH ANNIVERSARY

Looking down over Laguna Beach,
they sit on the park bench,
eating sandwiches and drinking wine.

They are not alone.
Their disappointment sits between them
like a quiet child.

They chew politely,
smiling occasionally at each other
as they reach into the bag of potato chips.

20 years. She remembers her boyfriend Pierre,
the guy he stole her away from
with his flirty talk and confident chin.

He was a good-looking chap, that Pierre.
She wonders what ever happened to him.
He pulls out some macaroni salad and a fork.

They smile at each other. He remembers his wife
as she looked the day they met, her white bikini, the sheer
sarong covering that dancer's ass and those shapely legs.

They shared a beer over the keg while Pierre was out
surfing with his pals. *Why would anyone leave a girl*

like this alone by the keg? he remembers thinking.

They did some beer bongs, some close talking
and casual touching. He looked into her eyes,
those dark brown orbs seeming to throb there in her head.

He felt his dick swell in his trunks—
a boner from merely looking at her.
That was 20 years ago.

Now they sit on the bench and eat.
She points to the corner of his mouth.
He has some mustard there.

He wipes it away and watches
as she shoves her hero into her mouth.
They drink their wine in silence.

And as the surf thunders below them,
a little girl begins to cry, her sandcastle
having been washed away by the tide.

FACE IT, MAN

Your wife's a dud.
Yes, I know she has beautiful lips
but she doesn't even *use* them
if you know what I mean.

Yes, yes, exotic eyes
which watch you like a jailor.

Look,
let's take stock:
she wears a pad
even when she's not on her period
in case you make her laugh
or if she sneezes;
she hasn't worn a bikini since your honeymoon
in 1986—
nothing but one-pieces
like a lifeguard,
only she's not guarding your life;
her only thongs
are the ones she bought in Hawaii
because the sand was miserable
on her feet;
the only sex you have is
sex you initiate
and by initiate, I mean

you get yourself worked up
then you attempt to seduce her
then you beg
then she acquiesces
but only after she pees
and only in the bedroom
lights off
and don't put on that sleepy jazz music
don't put on any music
but don't make all those
slurpy sex sounds either
and don't sticky the sheets
no porn
and no, she won't kiss you there
and the back door is boarded up
and what's gotten into you anyway?
Have you been staring at that Asian girl
down at the coffee shop again?
Oh, and would it kill you
to lose a few pounds?
And don't act like she's a prude
because every married woman is like this.
She knows because she sees them on TV,
and you remind her that they are on TV
because they are getting counseling
from the audience because their sex-life
sucks.

Anyway, I told him all this a couple
months ago
and I have not heard from him
since.
Some mutual friends
say he's in counseling,
so I keep my TV
turned on
in hopes of seeing how he's doing.

You Can't Dance

You want the brunette so badly
that when she calls you out
to the dance floor
you spring to your 2 left feet
and head out to join her.

And she can dance, and you cannot,
so you feel foolish, but it's 1am
and you are dancing with the brunette
so maybe you can dance, you think,
or better, maybe you can't, and she doesn't care.

WITH CAUSE

He had sex in
the milk cooler at the supermarket
when he was seventeen.

She was an eighteen-year-old
from San Pedro with dark hair
and dark eyes
and she was the sexiest thing
you'd ever expect to see
bent over the milk crates like that.

He was young then, and strong,
and he had the little thing by her hips,
her pigtails dangling like puppet feet
and swinging in the cold air.

And although
his ass was working vigorously,
it was cold and white and exposed
and a little old lady from Rolling Hills
looked in past the buttermilk
and saw his cheeks working away
and she screamed bloody murder,
and though he was able to finish
and zip back up before the manager arrived,
he was promptly let go, with cause,

though no one dared mention the cause
until now.

LET THE PUMPING BEGIN

My wife offers to let me help
pump her breasts for the baby.
I wonder to myself why a man
would want to pump his wife's breast
for the mere purpose of feeding a child.
I do not mention this to her;
I simply decline.

I can sense she is offended as she
turns away and covers them,
as though those glorious mounds
I have devoured milklessly
for over a decade
are no longer my playthings.

They are udders now.

I am to share them with the Boy,
he and I partners in the business
of milking Mommy.

I tell my wife that I want to
hang on to those last remaining
bits of her sexuality.

I ask her to imagine a world

where my penis is used as lunch meat.
Would such a dangling piece of food
ever again be a turn-on for her?

Or what if my nuts were
just a couple olives
to be placed in a martini
or atop a Greek salad.

Would she still enjoy them slapping
against her in the heat of the moment,
or would she grow dry and flip over
fumbling for some vermouth
and a toothpick?

She just stares at me as the baby
cries from his crib—
little bastard's hungry.

Let the pumping begin.

THE LADY IN THE CAT HAT

The lady never left her home
so we always assumed
she would be wheeled out
in a plastic bag one day,
her home taped up and condemned.

We waited for Hazmat
to pull up and cart out
years of trash and feces.

Turns out she was very
healthy and clean
and the reason she never
ventured out
was because a man had
broken her heart
and in the aftermath
she had married her cat
in a private ceremony
with her parrot presiding
and her two labradoodles
sitting in as witnesses.

When she finally did come outside
one winter night under
a clear sky and full moon,

we did not call out to her.
We just watched her lay
the dead husband on a tree stump
and begin the skinning.
She was fastidious,
even through the sobbing,
separating the pelt from the meat
with surgical attention to detail.
The grave was dug with a hand shovel
and completed in five minutes—
3 feet by 3 feet by 3 feet.

She laid him in there
with a deep, crying inhale of breath.
She said some things
we could not understand
then she shoveled the dirt back
over him. It was actually
quite beautiful there in the garden
under the orange light of the moon.

Today, as she strolls our streets
reading poetry in a hat
fashioned from the pelt of her dead love
we do not poke fun,
we just smile and nod
for a love like hers
should never be diminished.

IF I WERE MAYOR

If I were mayor, I would draft an ordinance
making you my only citizen,
and I would appreciate you so much
that I would never tax you,
and I would let you ride around town
in the fire truck, sirens on.
I would make sure the diner downtown
had a ham sandwich named after you,
and every weekend
there would be a parade in your honor,
and you would ride on the back
of an old DeSoto convertible and wave.
But the car would have to drive itself
because I would be marching alongside,
banging a big drum or showing off
on horseback while doing rope tricks
and playing the harmonica.
At dusk, I would play
the You Spangled Banner
on my trumpet
and, at nightfall,
I would launch fireworks into the sky.
And we would sit there together
for hours, holding hands
and sipping mojitos
in rocking chairs

on the porch of an old mansion,
as the bunting rustles in the gentle breeze
and the fireflies come out to mate.
And you, having been properly honored,
would tell me you love me,
lighting a fire in me that would burn
so bright God himself
would be forced to wear shades
as he sits in his lawn chair and smiles,
having very much enjoyed our show.

ON LIVING

My Whole Life

The leaden pull
of not enough—
it is a tiring load
and it causes
back aches,
and club foot,
and yeast infections,
and I've been
lugging it
my whole life.

BOYHOOD

It wasn't yellowing teeth
and a balding head.

It was not a befuddling
click in my hip or boredom.

It wasn't a wife in the bedroom
shopping by mail or combing the cat.

Neither was it the insurance contracts
stuffed in my pocket and signed
in triplicate.

It certainly wasn't a mortgage,
or the need for the proposal
by noon on Friday.

No, it was more
the tennis balls banged
against the garage,
the brutal wars waged
in my parents' backyard, four boys
acting as separate nations
in pursuit of one small plot of land.

Boyhood was tumbleweeds

and rattlesnakes,
storm drains leading to the ocean
tall enough for nine-year-olds
to walk through.

It was the snapping of bones in freak accidents,
grandmothers from Poland and Ireland
with stiff legs and sad eyes.

It was my grandfather in red flannel,
tugging at his oxygen tanks
while smoking his last cigarette.

Boyhood was chalk fields and dirt bikes,
nuns with halitosis, towering nuns
whose keys jangled like a jailor's.
It was priests who looked the other way
when the un-blessed wine went missing.

It was foreshadowing and apt,
and I am grateful for it,
all of it, fleeting as it was.

A Poem Ending in Cliche #2

You expect a curve ball at your knees,
slowly arcing in
at a lazy, seventy-five miles per hour,
but you get the heater at 100—
chest-high and whizzing.
You stand there motionless
or fall backward on your ass
as if shot by a sniper in the bleachers.
You hear the pop of the catcher's mitt,
and the umpire pronounces you dead.

Behind the plate, a fan hangs a banner
with a backward K,
that ugly label that hangs in ballparks
and scorebooks
like dead fowl,
marking so-called hitters like you
with baseball's scarlet letter,
telling the world
The bum struck out...looking!

You store the embarrassment away
like food for the winter,
and you pull a cliché
from your mind as if pulling
a ball from the bucket—

you swear next time,
regardless of life's pitch,
if you're going down,
you're going down swinging.

HOPE 1

Hope rises.
>Hope is beat down.
Hope rises again.
>Hope is steamrolled.
Hope rises again.
>Hope is stabbed in the gut.
Hope whimpers a small yelp.
>Hope is taken by the neck and throttled.
Hope dies a lonely bachelor,
his scant possessions donated to the truly desperate.

HOPE 2

It is the statistical equivalent
of a black ball hair
on a one-nutted albino.
No chance,
no hope,
no great achievement
flashing on the résumé.
No hope,
no six-pack abs,
no rainy-day fund,
no golden parachute.
No gold.
No parachute.
No hope.

I am defunct,
debauched, derailed.

And yet, even with all that
I am also unshaken,
unsinkable,
impervious to your arrows,
and, should you try, you'll find
you can't.

Because I am

broad-shouldered and fearless
and though the gods punched me out
years ago,
they haven't yet been able
to remove me from the arena.

THE AVERAGE MAN

The green shag and yellow wallpaper,
the smell of cat piss and bacon—
the average man would grab his trousers
and coat and make some excuse.

But he is far from average,
has never even flirted with average.
20 years ago, he had a small accident
with some Jiffy Pop.

His options are limited.

So today, he finds himself
walking naked
down her long yellow hallway,
his balls sticking and unsticking
to his thighs with each forlorn step.

He reaches the toilet, locks the door,
notices some corn caught in his teeth.
When did you have corn?
The man staring back at him
from the mirror has no answer.
He shrugs, removes the corn with
his index finger, pisses, flushes.

He notices something shiny
in the trash can next to the toilet.
Awesome! he mutters
as he lifts half a comb
from beneath the used Kleenex
and tampon wrappers,
dipping it into the toilet bowl
to remove a loogie
stuck to one of the tines
before using it to scratch an itch
on his left shoulder blade.

He returns to the mirror,
plucks some old meat from
deep in his cheek, sniffs it,
drops it onto his tongue and swallows.

He runs his fingers under the faucet,
brushes his gums with them.

He takes a deep breath,
unlocks the door, opens it
and walks back down the depressing hallway
to her bedroom,
where the best he can do lifts her leg
to scratch her ass,
ripping out a giant fart as he enters.

The average man
would buckle under the weight,
but, as you may already have gleaned,
the average man
may be the title of this poem,
but he certainly is not its subject.

THE PEOPLE LOOK LIKE FLOWERS AT LAST

the
people look
like flowers
at last
but my mind has
become a heavy
boot and it
tramples about
with a mighty
apathy.
and you are there,
a daffodil
flat on your
back
and my ex
a rhododendron
dead
atop the grass
and even my delicate
grandmother, precious
rose, petal-less
and limp.

THE OLD MAN UP THE STREET

He bought the most beautiful home in town
with its blue-green garden
and giant windows overlooking the sea.

We watched him spend hours
the day he moved in
pulling up plants and busting glass,
planting weeds
and hammering holes into his walls.

He drove his sedan into the pool
and poured soap into the Jacuzzi.
He spent that first night
watching it bubble like sea foam
while he sat on his roof laughing,
drinking whiskey and trolling songs
about the sea.

A hearse pulled up one day
and we thought he'd died,
but he got out of the driver's seat
holding a hacksaw,
and spent the weekend cutting away,
removing the long top so he could
look at the sky while he drove.

You could see him
swerving through town on a Sunday,
his long, white hair blowing in the wind,
churchgoers and animals
scurrying for safety.

So it really was no surprise
the day the authorities arrived
to take him away.

Apparently, the old man
had decided to do himself in,
drawing a warm bath
and taking a razor blade to his shins.
When they pulled him from the tub
he was laughing,
terribly pruned but alive.

And sometimes, late at night,
you can hear that old house
whistle and groan,
an ancient ship in a dark harbor
waiting patiently for the skipper to return.

On Dying

My Final Day

To the long list
of vainglorious managers,
those self-centered assholes
who jack off
into the mirror
and sport tattoos
that say *Manpower*—
I will miss none of you.

To My Gentlemanly Bosses

Based on the feedback I've received
about my poetry, I should be spending
my time sucking whiskey from the bottle
on an old sofa in some run-down shack
outside of Lynchburg, Tennessee,
bending occasionally to sniff a line of coke
or kiss some skank's herped cunt,
instead of writing these hopeless lines
of lousy, steaming, beer-shit verse.

So, I put down my pen, take a job
selling insurance
in sterile Irvine, California,
smiling my shiny retail smile by day,
drinking milk with my pizza
and saying all the witty things
my bosses have come to expect.

But at night, as my bosses ready themselves
for bed, flossing and rinsing their mouths
with mouthwash before finally
brushing their teeth and slipping into
their satin pajamas, just as their dentists
and mommies taught them, I am slowly
slipping away into the land of feedback,
where the whiskey flows like wine,

and the hookers are manifold. As they
dream of quarterly bonuses and mistresses,
I am writing of this dark world
in which I find myself,
the one where carnival music rides
the fog through the trees,
where fistfights and gunshots
are always breaking the doldrums,
the one where true life exists.

So, here's the deal, gentlemen—
when we are dead and buried
and your white limousines
are searching me out,
your people scouring
the clean streets of heaven
in hopes of finding me
in some gutter
so you can bitch me out
for not making the final meeting
on the big-money Montgomery deal,
you should know that my soul
has gone somewhere else entirely
and chances are
your driver won't take you there.

ANTS IN THE CRAPPER

The queen's highway runs
through my john
and I'm sitting there on the pot
watching the little bastards
chase their black mother across the tile
and up the legs of the trash can
and back down inside
where my half-eaten bologna sandwich
sits stinking up the joint.

I keep the Raid at my side like
a six-shooter and I'm letting the fuckers
have it. They flip over
and shake their little arms at me
like pissed-off senior citizens
I knocked down in the crosswalk,
so I give it to them again
and now they're just lying there
like drunks, defeated with
no queen and no hope.

I finish my business
and use my thumb on the straggling
little latecomers
and once I've checked
to make sure it's all done,

I flush and exit. Outside,
my wife is brushing her teeth
in front of the mirror
and she gasps as I open the door,
Jesus! she says. *What died in there?*

Eating My Uncle's Egg McMuffin Hours After He Died

I carried that Egg McMuffin around
with me like I was holding my uncle's hand.
It was cool and solid, but not of this world.

That lousy McMuffin—
sausage, egg, cheese and bread—
it became more than its parts.

It was something
from another realm,
something rank and memorable.

That horrid concoction
had become the food
of Death himself and I ate it cold—

the way truth comes to a man,
the way life educates a man, cold as
Death's curt voice as he whispers your name.

I chewed it like a cannibal, like a man
eating his uncle. All around,
people were talking with one another,

laughing as if a man had never died,

as if Life's filthy affair with Death
was not known to them.

I ate that Egg McMuffin whole until
it was just a greasy wrapper—
then I barfed all over the waiting room.

Not a delicate upchuck, but a fire hose
of puke, people scrambling for the door,
magazines used as shields, the whole

of humanity gagging and running away
from me—the sausage-spewing Godzilla
who had just eaten his uncle.

THE ORGAN GRINDER'S MONKEY

I've seen them in top hats and tails
their hair combed and tidy,
little trinkets and medals dangling
from their breasts.

But this one had wild, tangled
hair and he owned only
a very cheap suit.
I felt bad for him.
I had the same suit in my closet
and it always embarrassed me.

But goddam if that monkey
wasn't the liveliest, smiliest monkey
you ever saw! He just
danced and grinned his way
through hours of bad shtick,
collecting dollar bills
and banging his little drum.

He was a real money maker.

Then one day his handler
received some terrible news
and there was no more drumbeat.

Word went out and
the whole town came out
for one last show.
There, in a pine box,
was the liveliest, smiliest monkey
you ever saw, quiet and calm,
sunflower in his lapel,
little monkey hands
folded over his heart,
his glorious smile made still
for eternity.

I was there in my cheap suit
along with other men in theirs
and we shared a long cry for him
as he lay there motionless,
his cheap suit shining
beautiful and black in the twilight
on a hot corner
in the dead
of the saddest summer on record.

ANNIVERSARY

He sits in the kitchen near the Coleman,
whiskey bottle almost empty,
his face a grayish pall. Outside,
a Jesus Saves sign is flashing
and buzzing in red neon,
while below, the busy city streets are
an alarming reminder
that life moves on without you.

It is Wednesday and he is alone.

This makes four straight Wednesdays
pressed in on either side by all the other days.
The phone went off on Sunday, the heat
on Monday, the lights just three hours ago.

Inside these walls he had raised two children
and had been faithful to his Love. He drank
but did not show signs of addiction or decay.

Then his youngest died of SIDS
and his wife shut down
and would not speak or eat. Weeks
passed, and months, and finally
she ventured out, took a trip
to the cliffs in Palos Verdes,

and drove herself and their remaining child
into the Pacific.

He had buried them all,
his entire family in the span of 10 months.
Now, sitting there in the morbid red glow
he wishes he had prepaid his utilities,
had purchased life insurance,
or a gun.

Mostly, he wishes he had preplanned
the family plot, something on a hill
beneath an oak tree with views
of the city. Finding such places
when the hour is thrust upon you
is much too severe
and cannot be done well.

But how do you preplan such things
when you are 37 years old and your Love
is cooking macaroni in the kitchen
and the walls of your home are alive
with the sound of your children?

WRITER PASSES

As the guests arrive for my mom's party
they gather in the parlor—
little bent women clutching beads
and relics and poetry, emissaries
from the secret world of the illuminati.
Whispering, invoking, they troop in,
vigilant as nuns only sadder.
They offer gifts to my superior mother.
Know her long? one asks of another.
Forty years, the other replies.
Me, forty-five, a third adds.
They clear their throats
and swab their eyes,
seeing themselves beside her
in that mahogany box.
Their husbands cluster in the corner—
bankers, bosses and brigadiers.
They fold their arms and frown,
the way my dad did when mom
began drilling us.
Pass it on! she would bark
from the solitary barracks
of her nursing home,
Write! Write! Write!

Her old poems begin to fill the quiet room

exploding like bombs in the distance...
slowly advancing...
echoing through the trenches of our minds
touching, at last, the clustered men
who rise like monarchs
unfolding their arms,
escorting the little bent poets away—
leaving me alone with my mother.
I sit at her side writing of her passage,
one last gift for the
Supreme Commander of the Literati.

Won't you Please Invite me up for a Drink?

My dead kin walk my brain
spilling potato salad and whiskey.

My grandmothers are huddled
in the corner, sipping tea
and eating biscuits,
their subtle whispers
bouncing off the walls
like undercooked spaghetti,
while their husbands
smoke cigars and deal cards.

My uncle has his boots back
from before the accident,
that night a beer can sent his motorcycle
hurtling like a grenade through the April sky,
stealing from him his one true love—
the sensation of speed.

He is dancing up there,
if you can call it dancing, and the broads
are all drunk and bopping around,
and my other uncles are smiling,
and really, the whole lot of them
are drinking and dancing
and telling jokes—

good ones, colorful jokes,
jokes with punchlines
that haven't been heard
in the whole of time.

And here, alone in the corner of this bar,
I look around and see nothing
but dull, gray dust. I listen to
the tired knock-knock jokes
of dull gray men, grow weary
of listening to their stale pick-up lines.

So, I look back upstairs
and tell those crazy bastards,
I remember you! You are not forgotten.
And, won't you please,
because there is nothing down here for me,
please invite me up for a drink?

Baffling St. Peter, I Make it into Heaven

The poison in my beer
seems tastier than normal
so I order it straight
and the bargirl reaches down
and pulls the box from her
purse and she pours
the powder right onto my tongue
(tastes like sarsaparilla or wheat)
and I declare it so delicious
that I would gladly die for it
and I pull the box away from her
and eat the whole thing, carton
and all, then drop to my knees
and eat the delicious rat traps off the floor
and I head into the kitchen
and guzzle some detergent.

Boy, what a bar this was, Pete!!!

So, I begin opening the cupboards
and devouring everything in sight,
silver polish and glass cleaner,
Rumple Minze and 18-year-old scotch
and before I know it
I've discovered Saddam's nukes
and shoved them right up my ass

like suppositories and suddenly
I am glowing and I feel I've had
enough and I exit the bar
all lit up and giddy
and as I try to cross the street
I am struck by a bus.

St. Peter stands there, mouth agape
scratching his head. He checks his
clipboard, looks past me
to see the line beginning to build up.
He turns to the gates
where God himself is standing
with my kin
all of them bright as the sun,
smiling their godly smiles.

He turns back to me but
I am already gone,
having scaled the fence
during his confusion
to take my rightful place
there in the garden,
where I sit sipping
whiskey and lemonade
waiting for the tailor to come
and fit me for wings.

ABOUT THE AUTHOR

Randall McNair spent the better part of a decade drinking himself silly at the Swinging Door Saloon in Tustin, California, and was inspired to put pen to paper by a combination of Charles Bukowski, Billy Collins, Sharon Olds & the muse at large. His Poetry CV includes a BA in English (Creative Writing) from CSU Long Beach in 2002, the 2002 Key West Literary Seminar's Advanced Poetry Workshop with Sharon Olds, the 2009 Key West Literary Seminar's Advanced Poetry Workshop with Billy Collins and the 2019 Southampton Writers Conference 10-day Advanced Poetry Workshop also with Billy Collins. McNair's work has been published in both American and Canadian literary journals. He lives in Alameda, California, with his wife and young son.